Quick Cal

FOR YOUR STOMACH

CALLAN PINCKNEY

Vermilion

First Published in 1992 by Vermilion, an imprint of Ebury Publishing
Ebury Publishing is a Random House Group Company
Random House
20 Vauxhall Bridge Road
London SW1V 2SA

Pinckney, Callan
    Quick callanetics - stomach: The flattest
    stomach in only 20 minutes a day.
    I. Title
    613.7

    ISBN 9780091954826

Edited by Emma Callery
Designed by Clive Dorman
Typeset in Times New Roman by Clive Dorman

Printed and bound in Great Britain by Clays Ltd, St Ives plc

The Random House Group Limited supports The Forest Stewardship
Council® (FSC®), the leading international forest-certification organisation.
Our books carrying the FSC label are printed on FSC®-certified paper.
FSC is the only forest-certification scheme supported by the leading
environmental organisations, including Greenpeace. Our
paper procurement policy can be found at
www.randomhouse.co.uk/environment

WARNING:

There are risks inherent in any exercise programme. The advice of a doctor should be obtained prior to embarking on any exercise regimen. This programme is intended for persons in good health.

TO PREGNANT WOMEN:

Under no circumstances should any woman in the first trimester of pregnancy do the exercises featured in this book. During the second and third trimester do not attempt to do these exercises unless your doctor has actually done them to feel how deep the contractions are.

Do not just show your doctor the book. These exercises appear to be very easy, but looks in this case are extremely deceiving.

CONTENTS

INTRODUCTION

Welcome to Quick Callanetics. Whether you regularly practise a Callanetics programme using a book, video, or an authorized class in one of our new studios, or you are experiencing Callanetics for the first time, this book will give you safe, fast and effective results if followed properly. By using the basic programme set out in the original book, millions of readers have already discovered that Callanetics is a safe and quick way to change bodyshape to give the firm, attractive body we all dream about. Those mastering that programme have graduated to *Super Callanetics*. *Callanetics Countdown* presents a shorter programme for those with more demanding time schedules and if you are seeking a more gradual introduction to the basic Callanetics one-hour programme. *Callanetics for Your Back* is for those people with backaches or back problems. The book is designed to correct the problem or to make the back more flexible and to release pain. The exercises are also preventative for those who don't have back problems and never want to have them as the stretches and contractions actually strengthen the back. The appeal has proven to be international, with books now published in many countries around the world.

The huge success of the first Callanetics book brought a demand for videos; which include the original *Callanetics: Ten Years Younger in Ten Hours*, followed by *Beginning Callanetics* and *Super Callanetics*. Now we have the new *Quick Callanetics* series with three 20-minute workout tapes for the legs, stomach, and hips and behind. This book contains all the exercises, and more, as featured in *Quick Callanetics: Stomach*.

We all share common problems and have as our goal a strong, firm and shapely body, but our bodies also differ in various ways. A person may have a special problem in one area and much less of one elsewhere. Of all the problem areas of the body, perhaps the stomach is the most difficult to conceal. There are few things less attractive than that puffy bulge that ruins the line of a beautiful dress or that unsightly roll of flesh hanging over a belt. Swollen extra weight can create this problem at any age, but as we grow old, our stomach muscles lose tone and, if not maintained properly, weaken so letting the stomach muscles protrude. All this has made the manufacturers of corsets very happy. But this Quick Callanetics programme solves the problem in a fast, safe, and healthier way.

Sadly, many people practise the traditional sit-up as a way to condition the stomach muscles, not realizing that in so doing they are creating a terrific struggle against gravity involving other muscle groups. In particular, the back muscles come into play, putting pressure on the lower back which usually strains and prevents the stomach muscles from benefitting.

With Quick Callanetics, however, the body is positioned in such a way that you concentrate only on the stomach muscles. At the same time, you learn to relax the entire body, giving you total control over these muscles and permitting them to work at the level they are capable of performing at without forcing.

If you are not able to do the programme completely at first, don't worry. The next session you will find that the muscles have grown stronger. And as the muscles strengthen, they will work even deeper, and the exercises will become easier. Not only will your stomach flatten but your abdominal muscles will become stronger.

At first you will feel the muscles contracting just below the chest. As your muscles become stronger in that area, the contractions will be felt lower down. This process continues until you are working the muscles just above the pubis bone.

By doing these exercises, you will achieve other benefits as well. You will find your bust lifting as you are strengthening the pectoral muscles. Elimination will be stimulated and the programme can help lessen monthly discomfort among women. Tension in your neck and upper back will be reduced. Contracting (strengthening) will reduce a double chin and make the neck appear longer. Your spine will be gently stretched.

Note that the first few times you do these exercises, the neck could feel tense. This is because the neck muscles are being loosened. Simply continue and all of a sudden you will forget the tenseness you felt at first. Continued discomfort could indicate a medical problem.

THE ORIGINS OF CALLANETICS

I grew up in the deep South of the United Sates, Georgia to be exact, born of a long line of Pinckneys whose ancestors include the first Viscount of Surrey. They fought with William the Conqueror in the Norman Invasion in 1066. I found a life of well-bred tradition restricting, but not so the Pinckney fighting spirit. And I had to fight from the beginning for I was born with curvature of the spine caused by scoliosis and I had to wear steel leg braces for seven years to correct my club feet. It was only twelve years of ballet classes which helped to turn my feet outward.

INTRODUCTION

9

After two years of college I decided to explore the world, going first to Europe and then setting off to explore Africa, Asia and finally the Far East. I worked hard doing manual labour to make ends meet, and I further damaged my already abused body by carrying a backpack that almost equalled my weight, doing much of my travelling by foot. At 5' 1", I had always been petite. The starchy foods, such as digestive biscuits, and 40 cups of heavily sugared tea a day in England pushed my weight up to 129lb (9st 3lb). I developed a middle-age spread. Later my weight dropped to 78lb (5st 8lb) as a result of amoebic dysentery contracted during my travels. I lost muscle tone. I strained my back and knees, and my behind sagged and spread, making my outer thighs look like saddlebags.

Returning to the United States after eleven years, my physical condition was desperate. I had been told earlier by doctors that if I didn't have immediate surgery on my back and knees I could spend the rest of my life in a wheelchair. I could not allow this to happen, but I was unwilling to face the possibility of scarring from surgery. Within a year I could barely get out of bed.

DEVELOPING CALLANETICS

In the exercise classes I started attending on my return to the States I was shocked that most of them put a strain on the back. The movements were impossible for me, so I began to develop exercises to accommodate my physical condition. During my travels I had experienced a great number of exercise techniques, including belly dancing in the Middle East, and I remembered my earlier ballet training. Gradually I evolved a slow, gentle way to position my body into movements which protected the back. Instead of applying pressure to the lower back, I developed exercises which stretched the spine. At the same time, they penetrated deep into the body to reach muscles and shape and tone them with amazing speed. I learnt that the circular motions used in belly dancing loosened the pelvic area, gradually allowing movements in the sacrum area (lower back) where I had no flexibility left.

Each motion was delicate and precise, involving ¼ to ½ inch – tiny movements were all my body was capable of doing at the time. But these tiny motions focused the muscles in a remarkable way. In addition to correcting my physical problems, I noticed my behind pulling up and in, my stomach flattening, my posture improving dramatically day by day, my thighs becoming firm and youthful along with my inner thighs and underarms. I no longer wobbled when I walked and my arms did not jiggle when I waved. I felt totally comfortable in shorts or a sleeveless dress. My body was becoming incredibly strong and felt years younger. Friends noticed the change in my body. They wanted to know my secret. I showed them my exercises, and they also got the same, safe, quick results.

THE FIRST CALLANETICS BOOK

For the next eleven years I taught small classes of students who had heard about my exercises from their friends. My students had noticed remarkable changes in their bodies. For lack of a name for my exercises, my students named them 'Callanetics', and they also said it made their bodies feel 'ten years younger in ten hours'. They encouraged me to write a book. Finally, I called an agent. The book was a hard one to sell, I was told. I was not a celebrity, model or movie star. And it seemed that at the time every celebrity, model and movie star in the world had an exercise book on the market. Furthermore, I was not aerobic and aerobics were in vogue. But the agent was convinced by my exercises, just as my students had been, and the book was eventually sold to a publisher for a very modest advance.

Then came the crushing news. Of the few thousand books printed and distributed, over half had been returned unsold. I was too unknown. The publisher was to abandon the book and sell the remaining copies at cost. However, I knew that if I could only reach the public, they would recognize the value of my programme and reap the benefits of Callanetics just as my students had done. I did everything I could think of to bring the book to the attention of the public. When I went to Chicago for a final television appearance, magic happened and 14 months of hard work promoting the book paid off. As a result of that single television appearance, enough copies were sold in a week to place the book on *The New York Times* bestseller list in the number two position. It remained on the list for almost a year. That success has now been repeated in many other countries including Britain. I will be forever grateful to all those people who brought Callanetics to the attention of the public. And I am grateful to all of you who told your friends of the great results achieved through Callanetics.

CALLANETICS TODAY

Today, those of you who practise Callanetics are legion with more continuously joining the ranks. As this is being written, the word 'Callanetics' is entering the language through the *Collins English Dictionary* which defines Callanetics as 'a system of exercise involving repetition of small muscular movements and contractions, designed to improve muscle tone.' And what brought all this about? The answer is simple: RESULTS. The programme works for anyone of any age giving the fastest results in the shortest time with no injuries.

When I launched the original Callanetics programme, I introduced myself as a teacher. At the time the video was released I was 47 years old. Well, time marches on and I am now 52, and I am still a teacher. Now I teach Master Teachers who teach others. Callanetics has grown enormously from the days when I taught small, private classes in my small studio on New York's mid-East Side.

In November 1990, another major chapter in the story of Callanetics started with the opening of the Callanetics Franchise Corporation with headquarters in Denver, Colorado. Since the introduction of the books and videos, I was deluged with requests for classes and qualified Callanetics teachers. It became obvious that a programme for training and certifying instructors to teach Callanetics was needed. This was especially so in light of reports that classes were being offered by unauthorized persons with no assurance that the exercises were being taught safely or effectively. Now, however, you can receive qualified instruction throughout the United States and several other countries including Great Britain, Belgium, Mexico and Australia, with teachers who have been properly trained and are certified. You will find further information on how to find classes or how to open your own studio at the beginning of this book. I urge you to seek instruction only from those studios who document their certification and are listed by the Callanetics Franchise Corporation.

ADVERSE REACTIONS

I am very annoyed when Callanetics is attacked by those who have not tried the programme and cannot speak first hand of its safety and benefits. The same is true of other so-called exercise experts who feel it necessary to protect their interests by being critical of Callanetics. Rather than pointing out what other programmes can't and don't do and the injury they can cause, I have always maintained the positive value that my programmes can give. I have always said, 'My only competition is plastic surgery', and that is still true.

USING QUICK CALLANETICS

You may use this book in several ways. It is small and compact and can travel with you from home to work, on business trips or vacations, or wherever you choose to give yourself a quick reminder of the steps of the programme. If you are taking Callanetics classes in an authorized studio, you can use this book as a brush up source between classes. If you use an audio or video tape, this book will freeze the motion with a written explanation of how the movements work and will help you fix the precision of the position.

The book is divided into easy-to-follow sections. First there is the Quick Callanetics programme, exactly following the routine on the video. This is followed by some Advanced Exercises for those of you who may wish to push themselves a little further. Should you find the Quick Callanetics programme too difficult at first, the Build Your Strength section will soon enable you to work through the exercises with ease. Please note that some of the photographs in this book show you the ultimate goal of Callanetics. Do not worry if you can't do the same immediately – always work at your own pace.

Triple slow motion

The movements in Callanetics are tiny, delicate, gentle, and precise. They are done very slowly, as I have always said 'in triple slow motion'. Think of Callanetics as meditation in motion. In this way you reach deep, deep into the body to work the large muscles, as though working through them layer by layer. Never jerk and never bounce. Know how tiny ¼ to ½ of an inch is. Measure it! The movement is a pulse. If the directions call for 25 repetitions, think of it as 25 pulses. Do that amount of movement slowly and gently. Only when you are aware of the smallness and the gentleness of the movements, are you ready to do Callanetics correctly. You will then find your muscles will perform at the level they are best able to. Don't be upset if you have to take frequent breaks or if you can only do a few repetitions at first. You will become stronger in very little time.

No forcing

Because it is so important, let me emphasise that you must not force. If you are stretching, your muscles will only stretch at their capacity and you should not force them beyond that level. While you are contracting, or strengthening, the muscles, you should not be able to do more repetitions than the muscles will allow at that particular time. This prevents you from forcing the muscles beyond their limitations. Forcing the muscles can result in exhaustion or injury.

Do not – I repeat – do not be distressed or disappointed if you can only do two or three repetitions at the beginning, this is a natural process. With each session you will become stronger, and you will be able to do more. The most important goal is to learn to protect and respect your back to prevent back pain and to relieve back problems.

13

Curling up the pelvis

If there is one motion that is the key to Callanetics, it is curling up the pelvis, the link between the upper and lower body. Tighten your buttocks, and in triple slow motion try to move, or 'curl up', the pelvic area, as if you were trying to bring your pubic bone to your naval. Imagine there is a string attached to your leotard. Gently pull straight up on the string and your pelvis will curl up. This movement stretches your spine, and strengthens your abdominal, inner- and front-thigh, and buttock muscles, as well as your calves and feet, if you are standing. Gaining freedom in the pelvic area is very important because it affects posture, balance, and alignment of the body. It also loosens the hip joints and allows for more fluid movements. The more the pelvis is curled up, the deeper the buttock muscles contract and the faster the results.

Breathing

Always try to breathe naturally - and remember to breathe! Many people actually forget to breathe when exercising.

Counting

Several of the exercises include instructions to 'hold for a count of ...' You should count 'one thousand and one, one thousand and two,' etc. If you count aloud, the added plus is that you will be sure to breathe!

Think relaxation

Don't tense the body. Let the gentleness control the motion. By not forcing you will gain the full benefits of an exercise without exhausting the muscles or yourself. Exert the minimum amount of effort for maximum results. This is not to say you will not feel the exercises. You will feel them working deep in specific areas, without straining other parts of the body, particularly the back.

Commitment

Think, 'This is my time – a time I give to myself.' Think beautiful, soft thoughts; allow yourself to visualize and fantasize. You have done more than enough for everyone else. Now it is your turn. You will eventually attach the same importance to yourself as you do to the other elements of your life. Because it is fast and effective, Callanetics will fit into any schedule and can be done anywhere as it does not require special equipment. Just 20 minutes a day will produce results you will be extremely proud of. The other books in the series deal with the hips and behind, and the legs.

This programme is designed just for you. So let's get started. You'll be surprised how quickly you will see results and be capable of doing the required repetitions with ease. And remember, *gentleness* is the key word.

QUICK CALLANETICS

THE STOMACH EXERCISES:

• TIGHTEN THE ABDOMINAL MUSCLES FROM THE BREASTBONE TO THE PUBIS •

RELEASE THE TENSION IN THE BACK OF THE NECK •

• LENGTHEN THE NECK •

• RELEASE THE TENSION ACROSS THE SHOULDER BLADES •

• EXPAND BREATHING CAPACITY BY EXPANDING THE CHEST •

• LIFT THE BREASTS BY WORKING THE PECTORAL MUSCLES •

• REDUCE DOUBLE CHINS •

RELEASE TENSION AND STRETCH THE ENTIRE BACK •

PLEASE NOTE: This series of exercises may appear complicated at first. Please be sure to read through the text to get an understanding of what you must do before attempting them. The benefits will be well worth it. Don't worry about doing these exercises at exactly the level shown in the photographs. Do them at your own level, which is perfect for you. If you can only do five pulses at first, that is your level. As your muscles strengthen, your form will improve. Don't be discouraged, you will be able to do more repetitions each time you do the exercises. You'll be working the muscles deeper and deeper, and in no time at all each exercise will be a breeze. It is advisable not to wear shoes for any of these exercises; the weight of them is simply too heavy.

REMEMBER:

• NO BOUNCING OR JERKING •

• NO FORCING •

• WORK AT YOUR OWN PACE •

• ALWAYS TAKE BREATHERS IF NECESSARY •

• GENTLENESS IS THE KEY TO THESE EXERCISES •

Coming Up off the Floor

One of the worst things you can do for your back is to jerk yourself up off the floor and just get up. It is very simple to learn how to get up gracefully, in a fluid, easy motion.

❑ Lying on the floor, with your knees bent and relaxed, gently roll your torso and your bent knees over to the right.

❑ Now place your hands on the floor over to your right side, and, in triple slow motion, ease yourself up gently to a sitting position.

❏ Then, using the strength of your arms, bring yourself up to a kneeling position. In triple slow motion, take your left leg up, bent, to where your left foot is resting on the floor. Do not lock your elbows.

❏ Bring your right leg up. Tighten your behind and curl your pelvis up. Then gently, straightening up one vertebra at a time, return to a standing position.

Up and Down

THIS EXERCISE:
- STRETCHES THE SPINE •
- LOOSENS THE KNEES •

TECHNIQUE

❑ Stand with your feet a hip-width apart. Stretch both your arms up to the ceiling as high as you can. Tighten your buttocks, and curl your pelvis up (see page 14). Now stretch even more. Relax your knees—don't lock them—and keep your feet flat on the floor.

❑ In one smooth motion, gently bend your knees as much as you can, and lower your upper body towards the floor, with your arms reaching forward. Imagine you are trying to grasp an object on the floor in front of you. Your torso is stretching out and away.

❑ Gently swing your arms back, raising them as high as you can behind your body. Your knees will straighten slightly and your buttocks will raise with the motion of your arms going to the back and then up.

NOTE: When you have swung your arms back, as above, this will be one of the few instances where your pelvis will not be curled up.

❑ Just as you are about to reverse the motion to go back up to your starting position, tighten your buttocks and curl your pelvis up even more than you think you can. Keep it curled up until you return, arms once again stretching up towards the ceiling. If you have a swayback, tip your pelvis up as much as you can.

Repetitions
WORK UP TO 5

DON'TS
❑ Do not arch your back while stretching your arms up to the ceiling.
❑ Do not tense your knees or feet.
❑ Do not tense your shoulders or neck.

The Waist-Away Stretch

THIS EXERCISE:

- STRETCHES THE WAIST, SPINE, BACK OF THE SHOULDERS AND THE UNDERARM AREA •
- REDUCES THE WAIST •

NOTE: In this and the following Underarm Tightener, remember that as your body becomes stronger so you will experience no difficulty in curling up your pelvis. When this happens, you may keep your legs straight with your knees relaxed.

TECHNIQUE

❏ Stand with your feet a hip-width apart. Put your left hand on or just below your left hip, with your elbow out directly to the side. This is to protect your lower back. Reach your right arm up as high as you can, your palm facing inwards. Bend your knees slightly.

❏ Tighten your buttocks and curl your pelvis up more than you think you can. Try to reach with your right arm even higher, until you feel your clothing moving up your right side. This will stretch your torso even more. Gently lean over to the left as far as you can, keeping your right arm straight, and then reach just a wee bit more.

Stretch over more than you think you can. Because of my congenital bone problems, I can't go over as far as I would like. Most of my students can go over to the side much further than I can, and straighten their extended arm more as well.

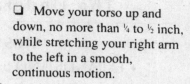

Move over to the other side in one smooth, continuous motion.

❏ Move your torso up and down, no more than ¼ to ½ inch, while stretching your right arm to the left in a smooth, continuous motion.

DON'TS

❏ Do not stretch over more than you think you can.

❏ Do not tense your shoulders, neck or knees.

❏ Do not forget to keep your outstretched arm as straight as you can, and as close to your head as possible.

❏ Do not bounce up and down. Your movement should be almost imperceptible.

Repetitions

WORK UP TO 75

❏ To gently come out of this stretch, do not stand up straight. That would put pressure on your lower back. Instead, bend your knees as much as you can and gently stretch your right arm and torso in front of you and then round to your right, in one smooth, continuous motion. Feel your spine stretching.

❏ When you feel that your back is totally relaxed and that you can't go any further to the right, slowly come up to your original, starting position by tightening your buttocks, curling up your pelvis, and rounding up your torso, vertebra by vertebra.

❏ Repeat this exercise on the opposite side.

21

The Underarm Tightener

THIS EXERCISE:

• EXPANDS AND STRETCHES THE CHEST •
• TIGHTENS THE UNDERARMS •
• STRETCHES THE SPINE AND PECTORAL MUSCLES •
• LOOSENS AND RELIEVES TENSION IN THE NECK
AND THE AREA BETWEEN THE SHOULDER BLADES •

NOTE: The more you can straighten your elbows, keeping the arms high and thumbs rotated and up towards the ceiling the more the underarms will tighten and the more you will loosen the muscles between your shoulder blades and stretch your chest muscles.

TECHNIQUE

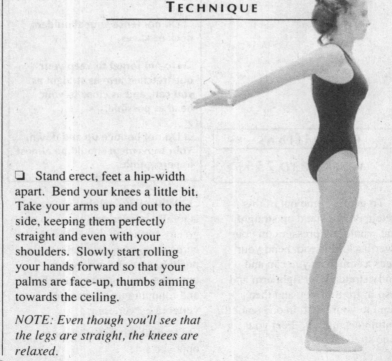

❑ Stand erect, feet a hip-width apart. Bend your knees a little bit. Take your arms up and out to the side, keeping them perfectly straight and even with your shoulders. Slowly start rolling your hands forward so that your palms are face-up, thumbs aiming towards the ceiling.

NOTE: Even though you'll see that the legs are straight, the knees are relaxed.

22

❑ With your knees still bent a little bit, tighten your buttocks, and curl your pelvis up more than you think you can. This is to protect your lower back. Make sure, too, that your spine is straight and your head is erect. Raise your shoulders to stretch your spine even more.

❑ Gently move your arms behind your back. Your shoulders will drop when your arms are taken to the back. Try to keep your hands even with your shoulders and your arms straight. Eventually this will happen. Without jerking, move your arms ¼ to ½ inch backwards and forwards. Always try to keep your arms up as high as you can, but without forcing them. Also, keep your wrists turned.

Repetitions

WORK UP TO 75

DON'TS

❑ **Do not uncurl your pelvis.**

❑ **Do not allow gravity to pull your arms down. Keep them up as high as you can.**

❑ **Do not tense your body. Especially remember your neck.**

❑ **Do not lock your knees; keep them relaxed.**

The Neck Relaxer No. 1

THE NEXT TWO EXERCISES:
- • LOOSEN THE NECK AND SHOULDERS •
- • STRETCH THE SPINE •
- • KEEP THE NECK AREA FLEXIBLE •

❏ Stand erect, feet a hip-width apart. Relax your shoulders and bend your knees. Tighten your buttocks, and curl your pelvis up more than you think you can.

❏ Stand erect, feet a hip-width apart. Relax your shoulders.

❏ In triple slow motion, roll your head down, resting your chin on your chest.

❏ Still slowly, move your chin over to your right shoulder as far as you can.

❏ Then aim your chin up towards the ceiling as high as you can, at the same time stretching the back of your neck up.

❏ Delicately bring your chin back down to your chest.

❏ Gently move your chin over your left shoulder, and then stretch it up as high as it will go.

❏ Bring it back down to where your chin touches your chest again. This is one repetition.

TECHNIQUE

DON'TS

❏ **Do not make any harsh or sudden movements.**

❏ **Do not hunch or tense your shoulders.**

❏ **Do not tense your jaw.**

❏ **Do not lock your knees.**

❏ **Do not stick out your stomach or arch your lower back.**

Repetitions
TO EACH SIDE

4

The Neck Relaxer No. 2

TECHNIQUE

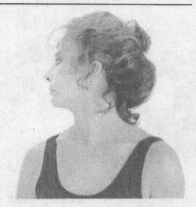

❏ In the same stance, with your body relaxed, shoulders melting into the floor, buttocks tightened, pelvis curled up, and knees relaxed, gently look over to your right side as if you were having a conversation with someone standing behind you.

❏ In triple slow motion, turn your head to where you are looking over your left shoulder.

❏ Finally, slowly move your head back to the centre.

Repetitions
TO EACH SIDE
4

DON'TS

❏ Do not tense your shoulders; they must stay relaxed, dropping down to the floor. Don't let them move up—as they tend to do naturally when you are stretching your neck up, if you're not thinking about it.

❏ Do not move your body or your shoulders.

❏ Do not relax your buttocks nor stop curling up your pelvis.

❏ Do not lock your knees.

❏ Do not jerk your neck as you move it.

25

The Bent-Knee Reach

For the benefits of this and the next two exercises see page 15.

TECHNIQUE

❑ Lie on the floor, knees bent, feet flat a hip-width apart, and arms at your sides. Relax your shoulders. With your head still on the floor, grab your inner thighs with all your might. Take your elbows out to the side as much as you can, and then aim them up towards the ceiling. This stretches your upper back muscles.

❑ Letting the lower part of your back be relaxed and melting into the floor, slowly round your head and shoulders up, off the floor. You will be rounding your nose into your chest. At the same time, bring your elbows out and up toward the ceiling even more, all the while grasping the inner thighs for dear life.

❑ Once your torso is rounded as much as possible, gently lower your arms to the side of your legs, aiming them straight to the front of you, about 6 to 12 inches off the floor.

❑ Gently, in triple slow motion, move your upper torso ¼ to ½ inch, back and forth. Totally relax your buttocks and lower back by melting them into the floor.

❑ If you feel discomfort in your neck the first few times, grasp your hands behind your head, letting your head rest in the palms of your hands, keeping your elbows out to the side.

NOTE: Be certain to maintain that fabulous round! If your torso falls back a bit, don't worry; it's normal. At first, most people's stomach muscles are not strong enough to hold the position in the photographs.

❏ If you continue to feel discomfort in the back of your neck after the first four times you do these exercises, attempt the Sit Up and Curl Down shown starting on page 41. If the discomfort persists you should consult your doctor as this could be a signal of chronic disc problems. Feeling discomfort in the back of your neck at first is natural, usually because of the stress of everyday living. Unless you have a chronic problem, this discomfort will disappear. You will then experience a sensation in the muscles at both sides of your neck. Be very grateful for this latter sensation as these are the muscles which make the neck look longer.

❏ If you feel strain in your lower back while pulsing your upper torso ¼ to ½ inch into your chest, it is usually because you are tensing your lower back muscles instead of letting your lower back be relaxed by letting it melt into the floor. If you do not see visible results after the first six sessions and your stomach appears puffy or swollen, it is possible you may have a medical disorder, and you should consult your doctor.

❏ To come out of this exercise, in triple slow motion, roll your torso down to the floor, one vertebra at a time.

Repetitions
WORK UP TO 100

REMEMBER: Take your breathers when you have to. Then you may grab your inner thighs with your hands, as in the starting position, and hold your rounded position. Then, before releasing your hands to continue the exercise, take your elbows out and then up, and then round your torso even more. Or, you may roll down vertebra by vertebra to rest on the floor—but remember if you choose this one that you must start at Step 1 again when continuing with the exercises.

IF YOU FEEL THAT YOUR ENTIRE BODY IS MOVING BACK AND FORTH ON THE FLOOR:

Lift your feet 1 to 2 inches up off the floor. Moving back and forth or in a jerking motion is a signal that your back muscles are trying to come in to assist your stomach muscles.

IF YOU FEEL THAT YOU ARE LOSING CONTROL OF THIS EXERCISE, OR THAT THERE IS A STRAIN ON YOUR LOWER BACK, EITHER:

Move your feet very slightly away from your body; or, take your torso down ¼ inch. If it still feels too difficult, take your torso down another ¼ inch.

REMEMBER: When you are first getting into position, your nose should always be aimed into your chest. Once you have built up tremendous strength in your stomach muscles, you can either continue to keep aiming your nose towards your chest, or you can raise your head just a little, aiming your face towards your knees while doing your repetitions or taking a breather. Never, however, aim your face up towards the ceiling. You won't be changing the actual position of your neck—you should only be shifting the position of your head a wee bit. Do whatever is most comfortable for you.

DON'TS

❑ Do not tighten your stomach muscles. This puts pressure on your lower back. They will certainly be doing enough work!

❑ Do not tense up. Just relax and let your lower back melt into the floor.

❑ Do not allow your torso and shoulders to sink to the floor. Keep them rounded off the floor as much as possible.

❑ Do not move just your arms or your shoulders or your neck when pulsing. They all move with your upper torso as a unit.

❑ Do not tense your buttocks. Relaxing them will take pressure off your lower back. They should not move at all.

❑ Do not tense your legs or neck.

❑ Do not jerk or bounce.

Single-Leg Raises

Most people don't realise that they can actually point their toes without tensing their leg muscles. In the following exercises, whenever one or both legs are raised, point your toes, but remember to keep your legs perfectly relaxed. This is a wonderful opportunity to start training yourself to relax different parts of your body.

TECHNIQUE

In these stomach exercises the raised leg should be straight up with the feet relaxed and the toes pointed towards the ceiling. As you become stronger, you will be able to lower the leg as pictured on page 30.

❑ Lying on the floor with your knees still bent, feet a hip-width apart, gently raise your right leg straight up in a vertical position, toes pointing towards the ceiling, grab the back of your right thigh with both hands, below your knee. Both elbows are out as far as they can go, and then aiming up towards the ceiling. If you have to bend your right knee at first, that's perfectly alright.

❑ Now, in triple slow motion, round your torso up bringing your head up off the ground first. At the same time, take your elbows out and then up even more to stretch the upper back. You are aiming your nose towards your rib cage.

❑ When you feel that you can't round any further, slowly straighten your left leg, raised no more than a foot off the floor. If this is too much at first either rest your left leg on the floor or return your left leg to its starting position, with the knee bent.

29

❏ Take your hands off your legs and extend them, straight out in the direction of your feet, 6 inches to 1 foot off the floor.

❏ Now you are in position to gently pulse your torso, in triple slow motion, ¼ to ½ inch, back and forth.

❏ To come out of this exercise, in triple slow motion—you have no choice!—gently bend your knees, one at a time, so that both feet are resting on the floor, and slowly lower your torso, vertebra by vertebra, until you are resting on the floor.

❏ Repeat this exercise on the opposite side.

> ### Repetitions
> ---
> **WORK UP TO 100**

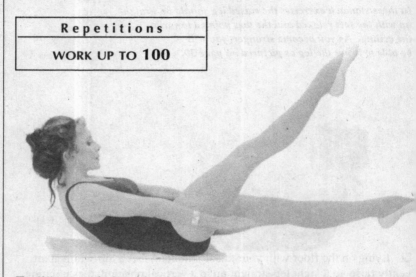

❏ When you feel comfortable with this movement, start to lower your upstretched leg ½ inch at a time. If you feel your lower back starting to take over—which is the signal that your stomach muscles are not quite strong enough—slowly raise your right leg back towards the ceiling, ½ inch at a time, until you feel no strain on your lower back.

NOTE: The lower one or both legs go down to the floor, the more your stomach muscles work.

IF THIS EXERCISE IS STLL TOO MUCH AT FIRST OR IF YOU STILL FEEL PRESSURE ON YOUR LOWER BACK:
Gently raise your upstretched leg towards the ceiling, or lower your torso ¼ inch towards the floor.

IF YOU NEED TO TAKE A BREATHER:

Bring your right leg up towards you, to where it feels comfortable, grasp it with both hands below your knee, hold your rounded torso position with your elbows out, and breathe deeply and naturally. If you need to, rest your left leg on the floor or bend your left knee, resting your left foot on the floor.

When you are ready to continue, return to your original position. That is, with the right leg straight up, foot relaxed and toes vertically pointed towards the ceiling. Note the position pictured is that which you will be able to achieve when you become stronger.

If you feel discomfort in your neck, grasp your hands behind your head letting your head rest in the palms of your hands, keeping your elbows out to the side. If you choose to return to the starting position, lower your upper torso to the floor vertebra by vertebra.

Gentleness is the key word.

DON'TS

❑ Do not tense your body. It should be entirely relaxed, like a rag doll.

❑ When you are in the starting position, do not pull your leg to meet your face, always make sure it is vertical. As you become stronger, the leg may be lowered.

❑ Do not let your back take over. Keep it relaxed. How much you can round your upper back depends on how stretched your upper back muscles are, and how strong your stomach muscles have become.

If you feel the exercise is getting too difficult, or your back muscles are about to take over, raise your upstretched leg ½ inch higher. The lower you can take your raised legs down, the more your abdominal muscles will have to work—but they must be ready for such an intense workout.

❑ Do not allow your upper body to sink to the floor, if possible. Keep it rounded as much as you can.

❑ Do not tense your legs, stomach muscles or neck.

❑ Do not forget about your elbows. Keep them up and out as high as you possibly can, while getting into position.

❑ Do not ever aim your face towards the ceiling; this puts strain on your neck.

❑ Do not tighten your buttocks.

Double-Leg Raises

TECHNIQUE

NOTE: When you begin this exercise, the legs should be straight up in a vertical position with the feet relaxed and the toes pointed at the ceiling. As you become stronger, you will be able to lower the legs as pictured.

❑   Lying on the floor, feet a hip-width apart, bend your knees up to your chest one at a time, and then extend both legs vertically up towards the ceiling.

❑   Grab onto your outer thighs, stretch your elbows out then up as high as you can, then round your torso up with your nose pointing into your rib cage at the same time taking the elbows out and up even more. Try to keep your legs straight but if you have to bend them at first do not worry.

❑   Once you're rounded and in position, let go of your legs and extend your arms straight out, 6 inches to 1 foot off the floor.

❑   Then gently move your torso back and forth, ¼ to ½ inch.

❑   When you feel comfortable with this movement, start to lower your legs ½ inch at a time. But only lower them as far as you can without feeling the strain in your lower back. Your legs should feel like feathers.

33

❑ If you feel that your lower back muscles are starting to take over, or your lower back is starting to arch, again, this is your signal that your stomach muscles are not yet strong enough to work at this level.

❑ Slowly raise your legs back up in ½-inch segments until you feel absolutely no pressure on your lower back, or your lower back does not arch, and then continue the exercise at that level.

❑ To come out of the double-leg raise, in triple slow motion, bend your knees, and lower your feet to the floor, one at a time. Then lower your torso, vertebra by vertebra. Totally relax.

Repetitions
WORK UP TO **100**

NOTE: There should be no strain on your body at all—your lower back should always be on the floor, not arched. It takes incredible strength and control to lower your legs and still have your body feeling like a rag doll melting into the floor. Do not force!

IF YOU NEED TO TAKE A BREATHER:

Grab onto your outer thighs with both hands, hold your rounded torso position, with your elbows still aimed out to the side, and breathe deeply and naturally. Before letting go to continue the count, round your torso, and bring your elbows up and out more than you think you can.

If your legs eventually go down as far as mine, for a breather, you will have to very gently bring them back up to a comfortable position so that you can easily hold on to your outer thighs

DON'TS

❏ Do not lower your elbows. They must be out and up as far as they can possibly go for the starting position.

❏ Do not allow your upper torso to be anything but rounded and up off the floor.

❏ Do not tense your body. Especially relax your legs and neck.

❏ Do not tense your stomach muscles.

❏ Do not let your lower back arch or come up off the floor. This is another signal that your stomach muscles are not quite strong enough to maintain that position. If so, bring your legs up ½ inch. If that's not enough, bring them up another ½ inch and continue until you have reached a comfortable position. Concentrate on letting your lower back melt into the floor.

❏ Do not tense your buttocks.

Open and Close

This exercise builds up incredible strength throughout the entire body. In ballet school, before classes, some students and I would do Open and Close for stamina, leg strength, and for a higher extension of the leg. At the beginning, the more you do, the lower your legs will go. Expect this—don't think you're not doing this exercise correctly if it happens! Believe it or not, there are some people in their seventies who can do fifty Open and Closes effortlessly, without breathers, and their legs remain at the same height.

As with so much of Callanetics, this is an exercise that must be respected. Most people with back problems have found that Open and Close has helped their backs tremendously—because they knew their own limitations and did not force the exercise. This means they stopped when they felt that the lower back was about to take over, and only did what they felt they could do properly at that particular time. Even though this is basically a leg exercise, it requires tremendous use of the stomach muscles as well. This is why, if your abdominals are not particularly strong, your lower back will inevitably take over—which is not what you want! Build yourself up slowly, and you'll soon find that another wonderful benefit of this exercise is that your stomach muscles also become stronger.

NOTE: If you feel you're losing strength, or your lower back is about to take over, lower your legs a few inches, or bend your knees as you open and close. Or take a breather. If you find that you're still feeling pressure on your lower back, you must discontinue this exercise until you have built up more strength in your stomach and leg muscles.

REMEMBER:
Height does not matter. Work at your own level. You may well find that to begin with you will simply be moving your legs across the floor. The photographs here indicate what can be achieved if you keep on working at Callanetics.

BUT DON'T FORGET:
Open and Close must be treated with the respect it deserves!

NOTE: This is a wonderful exercise to do at the side of a desk or sofa to re-energise yourself during the day.

❏ You should be totally relaxed when starting this exercise. Sit on the floor with your upper back against a sofa or counter, and hold onto it as if there is a barre above your head. (Some people use a sturdy chest of drawers with one drawer open in place of a barre.) If you have a barre, sit under it with your hands or wrists draped lightly atop it. In the beginning you will be holding on for dear life.

❏ Bend your knees and take them up towards your chest. Point your toes. Scoot your buttocks forwards 4 to 5 inches so that you are not sitting on your tailbone. Gently drop your chin. This will help stretch your spine more.

❏ Slowly straighten your legs although if you have sciatica, keep your knees bent, without locking your knees, pointing your toes up towards the ceiling as high as you can without forcing. You are sitting in a jack-knife position.

❏ In triple slow motion, open your legs as wide as you can, and then close them.

NOTE: It takes incredible strength for your legs to go this high with ease. Work at your own pace. Do not feel you should be achieving the same height immediately. You will be very surprised that by doing this exercise regularly you will quickly be able to achieve this height.

Repetitions
WORK UP TO 2 SETS OF 5

❏ To come out of this exercise, gently bend your knees in the closed position, bringing your legs in close to your body, and lower them to the floor.

WHEN THIS EXERCISE BECOMES TOO EASY:

Move your buttocks closer to the wall or piece of furniture, the more difficult this exercise. It is much harder to raise your legs when you are sitting that way just try one and you'll understand. The higher you can raise your legs, the more challenging Open and Close becomes.

DON'TS

❏ Do not be in a position where you have to worry about the object you are holding on to being strong enough. Always make sure it is sturdy enough to hold your weight before you begin. Until you become stronger you will be holding on for dear life.

❏ Do not over do it. If your muscles are not particularly strong, stop and take breathers, and gradually work up to a set of 10, increasing slowly as your muscles tighten and strengthen.

❏ Do not allow yourself to become breathless. Take as many breathers as you wish.

❏ Do not tense your legs, especially the knees; eventually they will be as light as feathers.

❏ Do not move your chin up.

❏ Do not tense your feet but keep your toes pointed.

❏ Do not force your legs to move more than they can.

ADVANCED EXERCISES

Once you have mastered the Quick Callanetics programme you may find you have time to add a few more exercises to your daily 20-minute workout.

Both the Sit Up and Curl Down, and the Pelvic Ease-Down and Up require considerable strength in your stomach muscles. Work at them gently, always taking breathers if necessary as you build up the repetitions. These are incredibly effective exercises for stretching the upper back muscles. Remember – gentleness is the key word.

REMEMBER:

If at any time you should find these exercises too difficult, stop for a breather. Always work at your own pace.

Sit Up and Curl Down

You will be working up to 4 sets of 10 repetitions each, lowering your torso only by curling up your pelvis. Each set becomes progressively more advanced. You must take a breather between each set.

For this exercise, 1 repetition = 1 gentle wave of the arms up and down. Try to work up to 10 repetitions for each set.

WARNING:

Be sure the back is always rounded. If it is allowed to straighten, pressure will be applied to the lower back

---

TECHNIQUE

❑ Sit up with your knees bent, feet a hip-width apart and flat on the floor, your hands clasped just below your knees. Put your head between your knees, with your elbows out to the side. Scoot your buttocks forward until you are not sitting on your tailbone.

NOTE: When you scoot forward (first one buttock and then the other), it is similar to doing the pelvic curl-up, except you do not have to contract your buttock muscles.

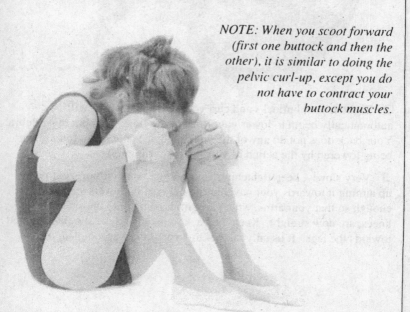

*Curling up your pelvis is what allows your torso to be
lowered like an old-fashioned ice-cream scoop.*

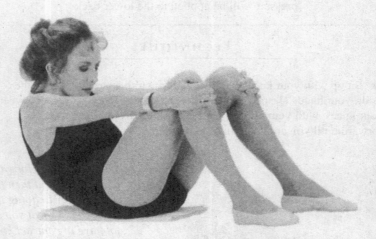

❑   Tighten your buttocks and curl your pelvis up, which will
automatically begin to lower your torso to the floor, vertebra by vertebra.
Your back does not do any of the work, and does not move (other than
being lowered by the action of your pelvis curling up).

❑   Very slowly, keep tightening your buttocks and curling your pelvis
up aiming it towards your navel until your curl-up lowers your torso
enough so that your arms, which are still holding onto the side of your
knees, are now straight. Keep the back rounded and the shoulders aimed
towards the legs. It usually takes 4 to 5 curl-ups to accomplish this.

❑ Without moving any other part of your body, let go of your knees. Your torso is still rounded and perfectly relaxed.

❑ With your arms straight, in triple slow motion, take them up as high as you can without forcing or losing your balance, and then back down to the floor in smooth, unbroken waves. Your body is balanced on the strength of your stomach muscles.

Repetitions
SLOW ARM WAVES IN EACH SET
WORK UP TO 10

NOTE: No other part of your body should be moving, except your arms, which will be flowing up and down.

REMEMBER:
If you feel you are losing your balance, that is your signal that your stomach muscles are not yet strong enough to allow your arms to go as high as you are taking them. Don't take them up as high on the following repetitions. You can also slide your feet a few inches away from your body or round your torso more towards your knees (or do all three!).

Notice how much lower the torso is from the curl-up after taking a breather.

❑ Slowly clasp your hands up more towards the top of your knees and take a breather. Because your torso is lower now from curling your pelvis you will need to clasp your hands higher on your knees. Hold your position, taking several deep breaths.

❑ When you are ready to continue, tighten your buttocks and curl your pelvis up even more. These curl-ups will round your torso more and take it lower. Let go of your knees and begin your next set of slow, gentle arm waves.

❑ When your stomach muscles become stronger, you will be able to take your arms up to where they are even with your ears.

❏ To come out of your second set and begin your third set, grab the top of your knees take a lovely breather, then curl your pelvis up even more, take your hands off your knees and continue your up-and-down waves with your arms.

> *NOTE: Because of your curl-up, you are now even lower and must hold onto the top of the knees.*

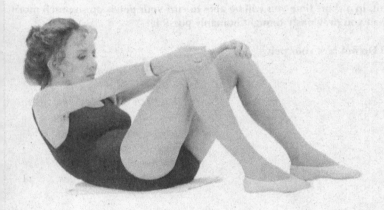

❏ To come out of your third set and begin your fourth set without moving your body, put your hands above your knees (towards your thigh), take your breather, then continue the routine one more time.

❏ To come out of this exercise, slowly lower your torso—even if you are so low that you only have to go down a scant few inches—vertebra by vertebra, tipping your pelvis up more than you think you can as you ease back to the floor.

REMEMBER:

At this level, you will probably feel that you won't be able to take your arms up as high. Raise them only as high as is comfortable.

DON'TS

❏ Do not straighten your back. Keep it as rounded as possible.

❏ Do not tense up; concentrate on relaxing. Your arms, gently waving up and down, are the only part of your body that is moving at all. Try to bring your arms up as high as you can take them, without forcing. If this exercise is becoming too difficult, don't raise your arms higher than your ears. The more your torso has been lowered to the floor, the less high you will be able to raise up your arms.

❏ Do not move your head up. Rather, you should keep your head down and neck relaxed.

❏ Do not forget to breathe naturally.

❏ Do not forget that after each breather, you should curl your pelvis even more by rolling your pelvis in towards your navel. Believe it or not, in a short time you will be able to curl your pelvis up so much more than you previously thought humanly possible!

❏ Do not jerk your pelvis.

*NOTE: This is absolutely the wrong way to do this exercise! If your back isn't rounded, this means you are balancing by putting pressure on your lower back, and **not** from the strength of your stomach muscles. Your back must remain rounded at all times.*

Pelvic Ease-Down and Up

TECHNIQUE

❑ Sit erect with your knees bent, feet a hip-width apart and flat on the floor. Scoot up your buttocks as in the previous exercise (Sit Up and Curl Down) so that you are *not* sitting on your tailbone.

❑ Place your head between your knees, and criss-cross your hands at the base of your neck. If this position is too difficult for you at first, you can place your hands behind your head.

NOTE: Your torso should continue to be rounded. You can always curl up more than you think you can.

❑ Tighten your buttocks, and curl your pelvis up in towards the navel, which will automatically begin lowering your torso towards the floor. Keep your pelvis curled up— never releasing it—as you curl up. Your torso will lower with each curl-up, one vertebra at a time.

❑ In triple slow motion, ease yourself down, vertebra by vertebra, until you lie flat on your back. It should take 10 or more curl-ups to accomplish this.

❑ Rest on the floor for a few seconds, your arms still criss crossed at the base of your neck.

❑ Tighten your buttocks and curl your pelvis up in towards your navel, then slowly start coming up, in triple slow motion. The head and shoulders come off the floor first and then lift one vertebra off the floor at a time, trying to aim your nose in towards your rib cage, until your elbows reach your knees and you are sitting up. This is the total reverse of all the previous steps. Always work at your own pace.

Repetitions DOWN AND UP
1

NOTE: Only attempt this reversal, curling slowly back up, if you are certain your stomach muscles are strong enough to support this position without your lower back taking over. At first, if you feel you are about to lose your balance, you will probably have to move your feet away from your body until your stomach muscles become extremely strong.

REMEMBER:

Many people's stomach muscles will not be strong enough at this point to attempt to ease back up. This is much harder as you must now lift the weight of your torso against gravity to come up. And when you do attempt to ease back up, you will probably laugh—your muscles have to be lethal for you to accomplish this!

Don't mentally beat yourself up if you can't do it yet—I don't think even Superman could do this one it's so powerful! (Well, maybe he could if he didn't forget to wear his blue tights!) I must admit even I am shocked when I see men and women in their seventies coming back up with ease.

DON'TS

❏ Do not attempt this exercise unless you have incredibly strong stomach muscles—but practice makes perfect.

❏ Do not tense your neck.

❏ Do not forget to curl up—you can always curl up more than you think you can.

❏ Do not jerk or thrust your torso, or use your back to lower yourself down or to bring yourself back up. Only by tightening your buttocks and curling your pelvis up will you ease yourself down and up.

❏ Do not forget to breathe normally.

❏ Do not tense your legs. Relax—they are like feathers.

BUILD YOUR STRENGTH

The following programme has been devised to help you slowly increase your strength if you find the Quick Callanetics or Advanced Exercises programmes too much for you at first.

The Underarm Tightener, Waist-Away Stretch and the two Neck Relaxers act as a general warm up to loosen your body before moving on to the more specific exercises aimed at working your stomach.

Days 1-4

The Underarm Tightener

It may not be anatomically proper, but underarm is the best term I've found to describe the under part of the upper arm—the part that tends to get loose and dangling. This exercise will help to banish underarm goosh.

THIS EXERCISE:
- EXPANDS AND STRETCHES THE CHEST •
- TIGHTENS THE UNDERARMS •
- STRETCHES THE SPINE AND PECTORAL MUSCLES •
- LOOSENS AND RELIEVES TENSION IN
THE NECK AND THE AREA BETWEEN
THE SHOULDER BLADES •

❑ Sit on the edge of a chair or sofa, keeping your back straight and your feet resting comfortably on the floor. Do not lean back. Take your arms out to the sides. Try to keep them straight, at about shoulder level.

DON'TS

❑ Do not jerk your arms back and forth.

❑ Do not arch your back or stick out your stomach.

❑ Do not lock your elbows.

❑ Do not tense your shoulders.

❑ Slowly, turn your hands forward and over, so that the backs of your hands are facing the floor, and your palms and thumbs are facing upward.

❑ Leaning forward, very gently bring your arms back as far as you can, keeping them as straight as possible, as if you were trying to get the backs of your hands to touch. Try to hold your arms as high as possible as you take them back.

51

❏ Gently, in triple slow motion, move your arms ¼ to ½ inch closer together and back, being very careful to avoid any jerky motions. After a few of these movements, gravity will pull your arms down and your head and shoulders forward from wherever you started. Be conscious of this, and try to return them to the proper position.

❏ You may not be able to keep your elbows entirely straight at first. (Some people are never able to straighten their arms fully; that's perfectly all right.)

Repetitions			
Day 1	Day 2	Day 3	Day 4
25	30	40	50

❏ Upon completion, gently release your arms by bending your elbows and, in triple slow motion, return to the starting position.

The Waist-Away Stretch

An alternative to wearing cinchers and corsets!

THIS EXERCISE:

- STRETCHES THE WAIST, SPINE, BACK OF THE
  SHOULDERS, AND UNDERARM AREA •
  - REDUCES WAIST SIZE •

TECHNIQUE

❏ Sit up straight in an armchair
and allow your left arm to rest on
the arm of the chair. (If you don't
have an armchair, simply rest your
left palm beside you on the seat of
the chair.)

❏ Keeping the spine straight,
slowly stretch your right arm up to
the ceiling, palm facing inward.
Try to keep your arm by your ear.
You should feel the stretch from
your waist right up to your
underarm. Now, stretch up and try
to reach even higher. Then start
reaching over gently to the left
side, trying to move your upper
body and arm in the same
direction, as if they were welded
together.

53

S
T
O
M
A
C
H

❏ When you have reached over to the side as far as you can, move ¼ to ½ inch over and back. You should not be making any bouncing or jerking movements, and remember—move in triple slow motion.

❏ To reverse sides, or to come out of this exercise, slowly lower your arm and straighten your spine, until you have returned to the original position.

NOTE: If you feel any discomfort in your lower back, or if you have a swayback, you may want to try this exercise with your arms and torso bending slightly forward.

DON'TS

❏ Do not bounce.

❏ Do not tense your shoulders or neck.

❏ Do not arch your lower back or stick out your stomach.

Repetitions TO EACH SIDE			
Day1	Day2	Day3	Day4
25	30	40	50

The Neck Relaxer No. 1

A way to unlock tension.

THIS EXERCISE:
- LOOSENS THE NECK AND SHOULDERS •
- STRETCHES THE SPINE •
- KEEPS THE NECK AREA FLEXIBLE •

TECHNIQUE

❑ Sit up straight in a chair or stand erect, feet a hip-width apart, knees bent, feet forward. Relax your shoulders—so much so that you feel they are sinking into the floor. Relax your entire body, being careful not to arch your back or stick out your buttocks.

❑ In triple slow motion, stretch your neck up. . At the same time, lower your chin until it is resting on your chest. Relax your jaw. Relax your shoulders, and try to keep them even and back.

❑ Gently, leading with your chin, move your head towards your right shoulder until your nose is even with the middle of your shoulder. Now, look over your shoulder as far as possible, trying to stretch your neck even more. Hold for a slow count of 5.

DON'TS

❑ Do not make any sharp or sudden movements; extreme moves can injure your neck.

❑ Do not hunch or tense your shoulders.

❑ Do not tense your jaw; it may help to keep your lips slightly apart.

❑ Do not lock your knees.

❑ Do not stick out your buttocks or stomach.

❑ Neck still stretched, slowly bring your chin back down to your chest and move it towards your left shoulder in one continuous slow motion. Look over your left shoulder as far as possible, as on the right side, holding for a slow count of 5. Slowly, return your head to the centre. This sequence counts as one repetition.

Repetitions TO EACH SIDE			
Day 1	Day 2	Day 3	Day 4
2	2	3	3

The Neck Relaxer No. 2

Relaxation—plain and simple.

THIS EXERCISE:
- LOOSENS THE NECK AND SHOULDERS •
- STRETCHES THE SPINE •
- INCREASES JOINT FLEXIBILITY •
- RELEASES TENSION IN THE NECK
AND BETWEEN THE SHOULDER BLADES •

TECHNIQUE

❏ This exercise may be done sitting or standing.

❏ Sit up straight in a chair or stand erect, with your feet forward, a hip-width apart, knees bent. Relax your shoulders and arms.

❏ Stretch your neck up until you feel you can't stretch any higher. Look straight ahead and be conscious that you keep your jaw loose. Feel as if your shoulders were sinking right into the floor and as if a string were running from your head right to the ceiling, stretching your neck even more.

❑ Gently, in triple slow motion, turn your head as far as you can to the right until you feel a slight, comfortable stretch. Then, very slowly and in one continuous motion, move it to the left. Try to look over your shoulders, but be sure that you don't rotate them; they should remain facing front. A movement to both sides counts as one repetition.

DON'TS

❑ **Do not turn your body or rotate your shoulders.**

❑ **Do not lock your knees.**

❑ **Do not tense your neck or shoulders.**

❑ **Do not stick out your buttocks or your stomach.**

Repetitions			
TO EACH SIDE			
Day 1	Day 2	Day 3	Day 4
2	2	3	3

The Bent-Knee Reach

You'll never do another sit-up.

THESE EXERCISES:
- STRENGTHEN ALL FOUR GROUPS OF THE ABDOMINAL MUSCLES •
- LIFT THE BREASTS BY STRENGTHENING THE SUPPORT MUSCLES •
- REDUCE TENSION IN THE NECK AND UPPER BACK •
- INCREASE FLEXIBILITY OF THE ENTIRE BACK •
- REDUCE A DOUBLE CHIN AND MAKE THE NECK APPEAR LONGER •
- ASSIST IN REGULATING ELIMINATION •
- HELP TO CONTROL APPETITE (FOR MOST PEOPLE) •
- HELP LESSEN MONTHLY DISCOMFORT FOR WOMEN •

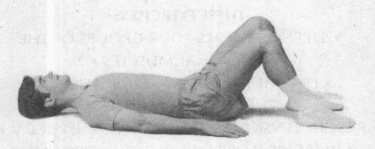

❏ Lie on the floor, your entire body relaxed, knees bent, your feet flat on the floor a hip-width apart, a comfortable distance from your buttocks.

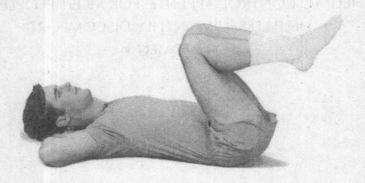

❏ One at a time, bring both knees to your chest. Then, clasp your hands behind your head, just above the neck, and cradle your head in the palms of your hands. Take your elbows out to the sides as much as possible. Do not aim your elbows toward your legs, as this may put too much pressure on your neck.

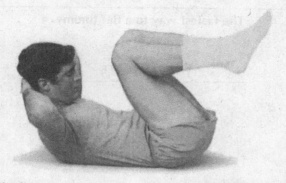

❑ In triple slow motion, gently round your head and shoulders off the floor, curling your upper torso and aiming your nose into your chest. When you can't round any more, gently move your upper torso ¼ to ½ inch forwards and back, within this rounded position.

❑ To come out of this position, when repetitions are complete or if you need to take a breather, return your torso to the floor in triple slow motion, vertebra by vertebra. Then, one at a time, lower your legs to the floor with knees bent.

❑ You can take a breather at any point. To continue, return to the original starting position, making sure your head, shoulders. and upper torso round up gently off the floor.

DON'TS

❑ **Do not rock your entire body back and forth.**

❑ **Do not tighten your buttocks.**

❑ **Do not bounce your head or aim it up towards the ceiling.**

❑ **Do not hold in your stomach muscles.**

❑ **Do not hold your breath.**

❑ **Do not lift just your head first.**

NOTE: As you progress through Days 1-30, this exercise will work the entire length of your stomach muscles. You will feel it in different places, with what has best been described as a feeling of 'working the muscles in layers, deeper and deeper'.

Repetitions			
Day 1	Day 2	Day 3	Day 4
25	**30**	**35**	**40**

Single-Leg Raises

The fastest way to a flat tummy.

TECHNIQUE

❏ Lie on the floor, with your knees bent, your feet flat on the floor, a hip-width apart, as close to your buttocks as is comfortable

❏ Raise up your right leg, perpendicular to your body, allowing the knee to remain bent. Be conscious of keeping your leg and toes relaxed.

❏ Keeping your head on the floor, grasp your right leg firmly, with both hands, behind the thigh, aiming your elbows out to the sides as far as possible. Then point your elbows up as high as possible towards the ceiling.

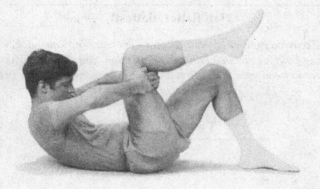

❑ Still grasping your leg firmly, in triple slow motion, round your head and upper torso off the floor, trying to aim your nose toward your chest. Slowly, move your upper body ¼ to ½ inch forward and back, within the rounded position.

❑ In triple slow motion, return your torso to the floor, one vertebra at a time. Then, slowly, lower the raised leg to the starting position.

❑ Repeat on the other side. Take breathers when necessary. You will only be able to move ¼ of an inch. This exercise is not about how high you can move, but how rounded you can keep your upper body. Keep your raised leg as perpendicular to the floor as possible.

NOTE: It is very important to learn to relax your entire body when doing this exercise to ensure that you do not try to use your back muscles to compensate for weak stomach muscles.

DON'TS

❑ **Do not tense your toes, knees, or legs.**

❑ **Do not bring the raised leg toward your head, but, rather, round your body toward your leg.**

❑ **Do not rock your body back and forth.**

❑ **Do not jerk up your head.**

❑ **Do not aim your torso toward the ceiling.**

❑ **Do not tense your stomach.**

❑ **Do not tighten your buttocks.**

Repetitions TO EACH SIDE			
Day1	Day2	Day3	Day4
25	30	35	40

Double-Leg Raises

Flat, flatter, flattest!

NOTE: To avoid putting any unnecessary pressure on your back, when raising both legs from a lying down position, you should always remember to bend your knees first and raise them one at a time, before you straighten your legs.

TECHNIQUE

❏ Lie on the floor, your entire body relaxed, knees bent, your feet flat on the floor a hip-width apart, a comfortable distance from the buttocks.

❏ One at a time, bring your knees to your chest. Grasp the backs of your thighs, aiming your elbows out to the sides as far as possible. Then point your elbows up as high as possible towards the ceiling.

DON'TS

❏ Do not lift up your legs without bending your knees.

❏ Do not tense your legs, knees, or toes.

❏ Do not move only your hands or arms.

❏ Do not jerk your neck.

❏ Do not rock your body back and forth.

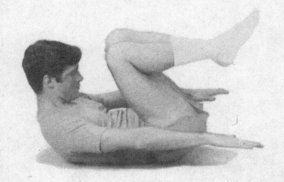

❏ Still holding on to your thighs, in triple slow motion, gently round your head and shoulders off the floor, extending your elbows even further out and up, curling your upper torso, and aiming your nose into your chest.

❏ When you can't round any more, let go of your thighs and extend your arms out straight by your sides, parallel to and a few inches off the floor, your palms facing downward.

❏ Gently, move your upper torso ¼ to ½ inch forward and back, within this rounded position. To come out of this position, when repetitions are complete or if you need a breather, return to the floor in triple slow motion, vertebra by vertebra. Then, one at a time, lower your feet to the floor, keeping your knees bent. You can take a breather at any point. To continue, return to the original starting position, making sure your head, shoulders, and upper torso round gently off the floor.

Repetitions			
Day 1	Day 2	Day 3	Day 4
25	30	35	40

Both Legs Over

To stretch the torso muscles.

TECHNIQUE

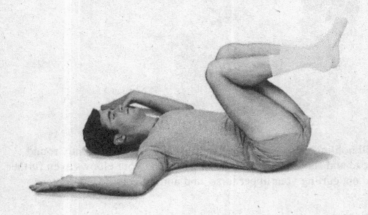

❑ Lie on the floor, knees bent, feet on the floor a hip-width apart; a comfortable distance from the buttocks. Your arms are out at shoulder level, elbows bent up at right angles, the backs of your hands resting on the floor.

❑ In triple slow motion, one at a time bring both knees in towards your chest. Take your right leg over to the right side, keeping the leg bent. Let your right leg relax. Then bring over your left leg, resting it on your right leg. Allow gravity to bring your knees as close to the floor as possible. Try to keep your shoulders on the floor. Hold for the count.

DON'TS

❑ Do not tense or jerk your body; these movements are fluid.

❑ Do not rush through this stretch.

❑ Do not force your legs to the floor.

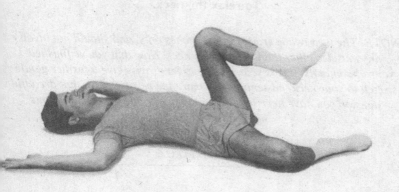

NOTE: Like Will in the picture, you may at first have trouble getting the backs of your hands to rest against the floor. You may also have trouble keeping both elbows on the floor. As you become more stretched, this will get easier.

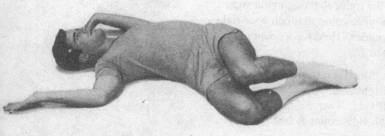

❑ To come out of the position, in triple slow motion and one at a time, bend your knees in toward your chest and bring them back to the centre. Repeat on the other side.

Hold for a count of... TO EACH SIDE			
Day1	Day2	Day3	Day4
30	45	60	60

Neck to the Side

To relax the neck.

NOTE: The next two exercises are stretches only, and should not involve any muscles other than those of the neck. Now that you've finished your abdominals, this is your chance to let gravity give a further gentle stretch to your neck, hastening even more the release of all that dreadful tension you have been holding for so long—and it's a marvellous opportunity to meditate.

TECHNIQUE

❏ Sit comfortably on the floor. Relax your shoulders.

❏ Keeping your shoulders relaxed and down, in triple slow motion allow your head to go over to the right, as though your right ear were going to touch your right shoulder. Hold for a count of 10 to 15.

❏ Slowly, return your head to an upright position and repeat to the left side. Two movements, one to each side, count as one repetition.

NOTE: When you lower your head to each side, you don't have to do anything but relax and let gravity do the work for you.

Repetitions TO EACH SIDE			
Day 1	Day 2	Day 3	Day 4
1	1	1	1

DON'TS

❏ Do not hunch or tense your shoulders.

❏ Do not make any jerky movements.

68

The Three-Quarter Neck Relaxer

To relax the neck.

TECHNIQUE

❑ Sit comfortably or stand erect, legs a hip width apart, knees slightly bent, feet forward. Relax your shoulders.

❑ Try to keep the feeling that your shoulders are melting into the ground as you stretch your neck up. Slowly, turn your head to the right until your chin is halfway between the centre and your right shoulder. Allow gravity to lower your head, stretching the back of your neck. Feel as if you were trying to touch your chin to your collarbone. Hold for a count of 10 to 15.

❑ In triple slow motion, raise your head and slowly return to the original position. Gently, turn your head to the left and repeat the movement, holding for a count of 10 to 15. Slowly, return to the centre.

Repetitions TO EACH SIDE				DON'TS

Day 1	Day 2	Day 3	Day 4
1	1	1	1

DON'TS

❑ Do not force your head down.

❑ Do not tense your shoulders.

69

Days 5-9

The Underarm Tightener

TECHNIQUE

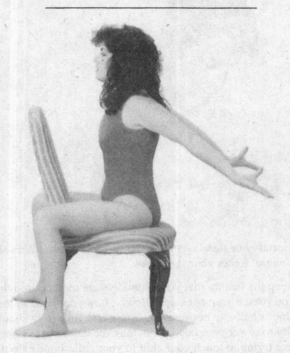

❏ Repeat the exercise as for Days 1-4, trying to keep your head and body as erect as possible. Hold your arms up as high as you can. You may find that, sitting straight, you cannot raise your arms as high as you did for Days 1-4. If your chair has a high back, you'll need to straddle it backward, as pictured, to keep it from getting in your way.

NOTE: The more you rotate your arms, the more your palms face upward, and the higher your arms are held, the more you will feel this exercise and the faster it will work!

DON'TS

❏ **Do not jerk your arms back and forth.**

❏ **Do not arch your back or stick out your stomach.**

❏ **Do not lock your elbows.**

❏ **Do not tense your shoulders.**

Repetitions				
Day 5	Day 6	Day 7	Day 8	Day 9
30	40	50	60	75

The Waist-Away Stretch

TECHNIQUE

❏ Stand next to a barre (chair back, table, or dresser, for example) with feet a hip-width apart, facing forward, knees bent and relaxed. Rest your left hand or arm on the barre. Keeping your spine erect, slowly stretch your right arm upward, palm facing inward. Try to keep your arm by your ear.

❏ Still stretching upward, tighten your buttocks and curl up your pelvis. Then start reaching over to the left side. Complete the exercise as for Days 1-4, bending both knees deeply as you come out of the position.

❏ Work both sides.

NOTE: At first you may have to do this exercise bent slightly forward, and you may not be able to keep the raised arm straight or by your ear. As you get stronger, your torso will be able to stretch over to the side more, and instead of just feeling the stretch in your waist, you will feel it from your hip to your hand!

DON'TS

❏ **Do not bounce.**

❏ **Do not tense your shoulders or neck.**

❏ **Do not arch your lower back or stick out your stomach.**

❏ **Do not lock your knees.**

Repetitions
TO EACH SIDE

Day 5	Day 6	Day 7	Day 8	Day 9
30	40	50	60	75

The Neck Relaxer No. 1

TECHNIQUE

DON'TS

❑ Do not make any sharp or sudden movements.

❑ Do not hunch or tense your shoulders.

❑ Do not tense your jaw.

❑ Do not lock your knees.

❑ Do not stick out your stomach or arch your back.

❑ Repeat as for Days 1-4. If you have been doing this exercise sitting down, now do it standing, with knees bent. As your muscles relax and become stretched you will find that you can stretch further without tensing your shoulders.

Repetitions TO EACH SIDE				
Day 5	Day 6	Day 7	Day 8	Day 9
3	4	4	4	4

The Neck Relaxer No. 2

TECHNIQUE

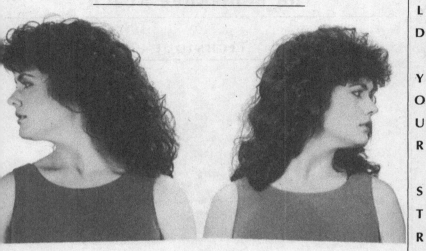

❑ Repeat as for Days 1-4. If you have been doing this exercise sitting down, now do it standing, with knees bent.

NOTE: As your body learns to relax, you will be able to perform these movements more smoothly.

DON'TS

❑ **Do not turn your body or rotate your shoulders.**

❑ **Do not lock your knees.**

❑ **Do not tense your neck or shoulders.**

❑ **Do not stick out your buttocks or stomach.**

Repetitions TO EACH SIDE				
Day 5	Day 6	Day 7	Day 8	Day 9
3	4	4	4	4

The Bent-Knee Reach

TECHNIQUE

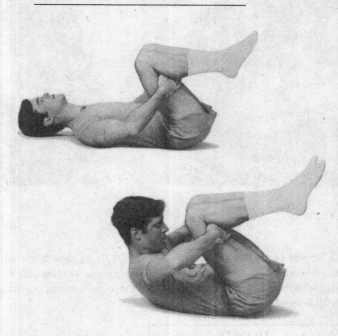

❏ Repeat as for Days 1-4, but this time, instead of clasping your hands behind your head, grasp the back of your thighs. Still holding on to your thighs, in triple slow motion gently round your head and shoulders off the floor, curling your upper torso until your nose is aiming into your chest. Complete the exercise as for Days 1-4.

```
┌─────────────────────────────┐
│          DON'TS             │
├─────────────────────────────┤
│ ❏ Do not rock your entire body │
│ back and forth.              │
│                             │
│ ❏ Do not tighten your buttocks. │
│                             │
│ ❏ Do not bounce your head or   │
│ aim it toward the ceiling.     │
│                             │
│ ❏ Do not hold in your stomach   │
│ muscles.                     │
│                             │
│ ❏ Do not hold your breath.      │
│                             │
│ ❏ Do not lift just your head first. │
└─────────────────────────────┘
```

Repetitions				
Day 5	Day 6	Day 7	Day 8	Day 9
30	40	50	60	70

Single-Leg Raises

TECHNIQUE

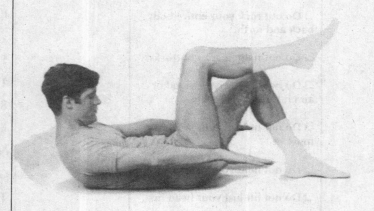

❑ Repeat as for Days 1-4, this time letting go of your leg and placing your arms straight out alongside your legs, parallel to the floor. Then move your upper body ¼ to ½ inch forward and back.

❑ Work both sides.

NOTE: Should you feel this exercise in your lower back, lower your torso toward the floor ¼ of an inch while continuing the exercise. If you still feel it, try another ¼ of an inch, and keep on lowering your torso in this manner until you no longer feel it in your back.

DON'TS

❑ Do not tense your toes, knees, or legs.

❑ Do not bring your raised leg towards your head, but rather round your body towards your leg.

❑ Do not rock your body back and forth.

❑ Do not jerk up your head.

❑ Do not aim your torso toward the ceiling.

❑ Do not tense your stomach.

❑ Do not forcibly tighten your buttocks.

❑ Do not move your hands or arms.

Repetitions TO EACH SIDE				
Day 5	Day 6	Day 7	Day 8	Day 9
40	40	50	60	70

Double-Leg Raises

TECHNIQUE

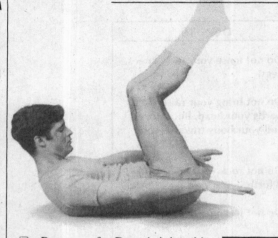

❏ Repeat as for Days 1-4, but this time, after bending your knees to your chest, raise your legs up, straightening them as much as you can. Do not force. After you have rounded up, release your arms so that they are straight out at your sides, a few inches off the floor, palms facing downward. Complete as for Days 1-4.

NOTE: In the exercises where one or both legs are raised, you will have the added advantage of stretching your hamstring muscles as you work on your stomach. On many people, this muscle is very tight, so remember not to force the leg to straighten. Be patient. Your muscle knows best, and it will stretch on its own timetable, when it's ready to and not before.

DON'TS

❏ Do not lift up your legs without bending your knees first.

❏ Do not tense your legs, knees, or toes.

❏ Do not jerk your neck.

❏ Do not tense your neck or shoulders.

❏ Do not rock your body back and forth.

Repetitions

Day5	Day6	Day7	Day8	Day
30	40	50	60	70

Both Legs Over

TECHNIQUE

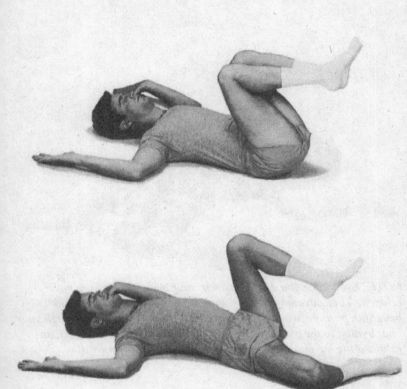

❑ Repeat as for Days 1-4.

DON'TS

❑ Do not tense or jerk your body.

❑ Do not rush through this stretch.

81

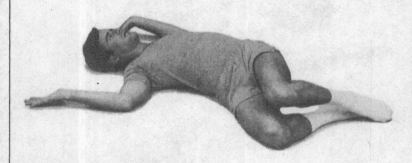

NOTE: Every time you do this stretch, your body will be even more relaxed. Take advantage of this time to clear your mind and think beautiful, positive, wonderful thoughts. Transport yourself through your imagination to the place you'd like to go most . . . a desert island, an exhilarating mountaintop . . . you decide. Relax and enjoy it!

Hold for a count of... TO EACH SIDE				
Day 5	Day 6	Day 7	Day 8	Day 9
60	60	60	60	60

Neck to the Side

TECHNIQUE

❏ Repeat as for Days 1-4.

DON'TS

❏ Do not hunch or tense your shoulders.

❏ Do not make any jerky movements.

Repetitions
TO EACH SIDE

Day 5	Day 6	Day 7	Day 8	Day 9
1	1	1	1	1

The Three-Quarter Neck Relaxer

TECHNIQUE

❏ Repeat as for Days 1-4.

NOTE: The more relaxed your shoulders are, the more of a stretch you will get. As you continue to stretch these muscles, tightness and tension will be released, giving you greater mobility.

DON'TS
❏ Do not force your head down.
❏ Do not tense your shoulders.

Repetitions TO EACH SIDE				
Day 5	Day 6	Day 7	Day 8	Day 9
1	1	1	1	1

Days 10-16

The Underarm Tightener

TECHNIQUE

❏ Repeat as for Days 1-4. But this time try the exercise standing erect, your feet a hip-width apart, your knees bent. Each day you do this exercise, try to keep your arms as high as possible, behind you, with your shoulders and head held back.

NOTE: When you first attempt this exercise, you may find that your head and shoulders round forward and that it is difficult to keep your buttocks from sticking out. As you become stronger, you will be able to stand more and more erect.

DON'TS

❏ Do not jerk your arms back and forth.

❏ Do not arch your back or stick out your stomach.

❏ Do not lock your elbows.

❏ Do not tense your shoulders.

❏ Do not lock your knees.

Repetitions						
Day 10	Day 11	Day 12	Day 13	Day 14	Day 15	Day 16
50	50	55	60	65	75	75

85

The Waist-Away Stretch

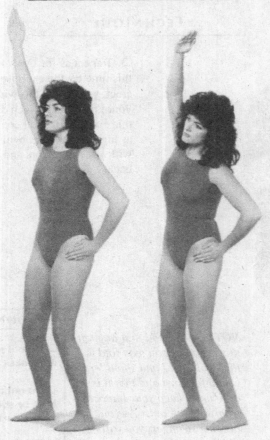

❑ Repeat as for Days 5-9, but this time, instead of resting your arm on a barre, support yourself by placing your hand just below your hip, your elbow pointing straight out to the side, if possible, and straighten your knees a bit.

❑ Slowly stretch your other arm upward, palm facing inward. Stretch up and over to the side, trying to move your upper body and arm together. You may bend slightly forward if necessary. Continue as for Days 5-9.

and bend your knees even more. Continue to stretch the right arm over, and continue around to the front, slowly extending your arm down and then over to the right side in a slow sweeping movement. Coming out of the stretch in this way prevents putting pressure on the lower back.

❑ Tighten your buttocks, curl up your pelvis, and slowly straighten your spine, vertebra by vertebra, as you lower the arm. Repeat the exercise on the left side. When you have completed the left side, come out of the exercise as above.

NOTE: At first you may have trouble keeping your arm fully extended and curling your pelvis up.

DON'TS

❑ **Do not bounce.**

❑ **Do not tense your shoulders or neck.**

❑ **Do not arch your lower back or stick out your stomach.**

❑ **Do not let your resting elbow point forward or backward.**

❑ **Do not lock your knees.**

Repetitions						
TO EACH SIDE						
Day 10	Day 11	Day 12	Day 13	Day 14	Day 15	Day 16
50	50	55	60	65	75	75

87

The Neck Relaxer No. 1

TECHNIQUE

DON'TS

❏ **Do not make any sharp or sudden movements.**

❏ **Do not hunch or tense your shoulders.**

❏ **Do not tense your jaw.**

❏ **Do not lock your knees.**

❏ **Do not stick out your buttocks or stomach.**

❏ Repeat as for Days 5-9, but this time, at the same time, curl up your pelvis as far as you can, to stretch your spine.

	Repetitions					
	TO EACH SIDE					
Day 10	Day 11	Day 12	Day 13	Day 14	Day 15	Day 16
4	4	4	4	4	4	4

The Neck Relaxer No. 2

TECHNIQUE

❑ Repeat as for Days 5-9, but this time, at the same time, curl up your pelvis as far as you can, to stretch your spine.

DON'TS

❑ Do not turn your body or rotate your shoulders.

❑ Do not lock your knees.

❑ Do not tense your shoulders.

❑ Do not stick out your buttocks or stomach.

	Repetitions					
			TO EACH SIDE			
Day 10	Day 11	Day 12	Day 13	Day 14	Day 15	Day 16
4	4	4	4	4	4	4

The Bent-Knee Reach

TECHNIQUE

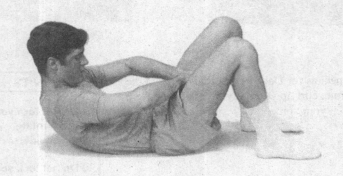

❑ Repeat as for Days 5-9, but this time keep your feet flat on the floor and hold on to your *inner* thighs with all your might. Still holding on, take your elbows out to the sides of your body as far as possible, then point them upward as far as possible before you gently round your head and shoulders off the floor, aiming your nose into your chest. Complete as for Days 5-9.

NOTE: Pay particular attention to your starting position. Done correctly this exercise builds muscle strength very quickly, and this will enable you to take your elbows out more and up higher, which in turn lets you round more and strengthen faster.

DON'TS

❏ Do not rock your entire body back and forth.

❏ Do not tighten your buttocks.

❏ Do not bounce your head or aim it up towards the ceiling.

❏ Do not hold in your stomach muscles.

❏ Do not hold your breath.

❏ Do not lift your head first.

Repetitions						
Day 10	Day 11	Day 12	Day 13	Day 14	Day 15	Day 16
50	60	70	80	90	100	100

Single-Leg Raises

TECHNIQUE

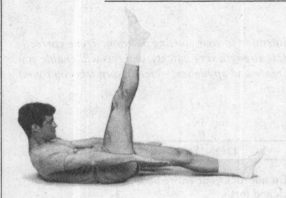

❑ Repeat as for Days 5-9, but this time try to straighten the raised leg as much as possible and try to straighten your other leg along the floor in front of you. Relax your legs and toes.

❑ When you release your arms to your sides, your shoulders may drop towards the floor a little. If you find this too difficult at first, keep holding on to your leg until you build up enough strength.

❑ Work both sides.

NOTE: Try to keep the raised leg as perpendicular to the floor as possible. If your stomach muscles aren't strong enough and you start to lower it toward the floor, the weight of your leg will activate your hip flexors, putting pressure on your lower back.

DON'TS

❑ Do not tense your toes, knees, or legs.

❑ Do not bring your raised leg toward your head, but, rather, round your body toward your leg.

❑ Do not rock your body back and forth.

❑ Do not jerk up your head.

❑ Do not aim your torso toward the ceiling.

❑ Do not tense your stomach.

❑ Do not forcibly tighten your buttocks.

❑ Do not move only your hands and arms.

R e p e t i t i o n s TO EACH SIDE						
Day 10	Day 11	Day 12	Day 13	Day 14	Day 15	Day 16
50	60	70	80	90	100	100

Double-Leg Raises

TECHNIQUE

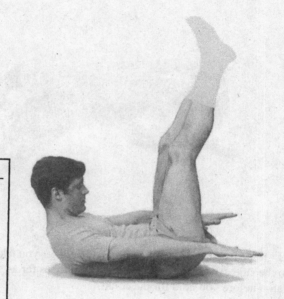

DON'TS

❑ Do not lift up
your legs without
bending your
knees first.

❑ Do not tense
your legs, knees,
or toes.

❑ Do not jerk your
neck.

❑ Do not tense
your neck or
shoulders.

❑ Do not rock
your body back
and forth.

❑ Repeat as for Days 5-9, trying to straighten
your legs even more.

*NOTE: Learn to completely relax your legs. You
do not have to tense them to hold them up.*

Repetitions						
Day 10	Day 11	Day 12	Day 13	Day 14	Day 15	Day 16
50	60	70	80	90	100	100

Both Legs Over

TECHNIQUE

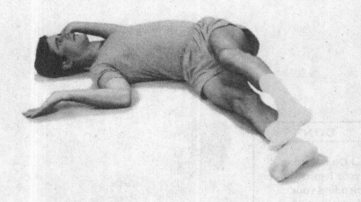

❑ Repeat as for Days 5-9, but this time, after you take your knees over to the side, try to straighten your legs—only as far as you comfortably can—before you hold for the count.

NOTE: Remember to keep both shoulders on the floor, and try to relax your entire body.

DON'TS

❑ Do not tense or jerk your body.

❑ Do not rush through this stretch.

❑ Do not force the stretch.

Hold for a count of... TO EACH SIDE						
Day 10	Day 11	Day 12	Day 13	Day 14	Day 15	Day 16
50	50	50	50	50	50	50

Neck to the Side

TECHNIQUE

❏ Repeat as for Days 1-4.

NOTE: As your muscles continue to stretch, you will be able to lower your head even closer to your shoulders.

DON'TS

❏ Do not hunch or tense your shoulders.

❏ Do not make any jerky movements.

Repetitions
TO EACH SIDE

Day 10	Day 11	Day 12	Day 13	Day 14	Day 15	Day 16
1	1	1	1	1	1	1

The Three-Quarter Neck Relaxer

TECHNIQUE

❏ Repeat as for Days 1-4, standing. Before beginning the neck movements, bend your knees, tighten your buttocks and curl up your pelvis to stretch your spine.

DON'TS

❏ **Do not force your head down.**

❏ **Do not tense your shoulders.**

❏ **Do not lock your knees.**

Repetitions TO EACH SIDE						
Day 10	Day 11	Day 12	Day 13	Day 14	Day 15	Day 16
1	1	1	1	1	1	1

Days 17-30

The Underarm Tightener

TECHNIQUE

❏ Repeat as for Days 10-16, this time tightening your buttocks and curling up your pelvis, your knees only slightly bent. Try to hold your arms up even higher than before.

NOTE: The stronger your muscles get, the more you will be able to curl up your pelvis. You will also be able to hold your arms straighter, and your elbows won't bend.

Because you will be able to rotate your arms and turn your wrists and hands further, you will be able to hold your arms higher while standing straight. This will work your muscles even deeper and loosen the area between your shoulder blades even more.

DON'TS

❏ Do not jerk your arms back
and forth.

❏ Do not arch your back or stick
out your stomach.

❏ Do not lock your elbows.

❏ Do not tense your shoulders.

❏ Do not lock your knees.

Repetitions						
Day 17	Day 18	Day 19	Day 20	Day 21	Day 22	Days 23-30
60	70	75	75	75	75	75

The Waist-Away Stretch

TECHNIQUE

❏ Repeat as for Days 10-16, standing straight and tightening your buttocks and curling up the pelvis even more before you start reaching over to the side. Try to hold your extended arm by your ear.

❏ Work both sides.

DON'TS

❏ Do not bounce.

❏ Do not tense your shoulders or neck.

❏ Do not arch your lower back or stick out your stomach.

❏ Do not let your resting elbow point forward or backward.

❏ Do not lock your knees.

NOTE: As your muscles get stronger, you will find that you can curl up your pelvis and bend over to the side even more. You will gradually be able to straighten your legs, still keeping them relaxed, and you will be able to keep your arms straight and by your ear. You will also become even more conscious of the wonderful stretch in your spine.

Repetitions
TO EACH SIDE

Day 17	Day 18	Day 19	Day 20	Day 21	Day 22	Days 23-30
60	70	75	75	75	75	75

99

The Neck Relaxer No. 1

TECHNIQUE

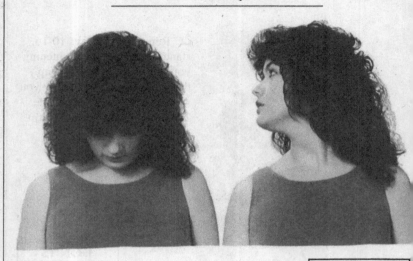

❏ Repeat as for Days 10-16, trying to curl up your pelvis even more, and without bending your knees as much.

DON'TS

❏ Do not make any harsh or sudden movements.

❏ Do not hunch or tense your shoulders.

❏ Do not tense your jaw.

❏ Do not lock your knees.

❏ Do not stick out your stomach or arch your back.

Repetitions TO EACH SIDE						
Day 17	Day 18	Day 19	Day 20	Day 21	Day 22	Days 23-30
4	4	4	4	4	4	4

The Neck Relaxer No. 2

TECHNIQUE

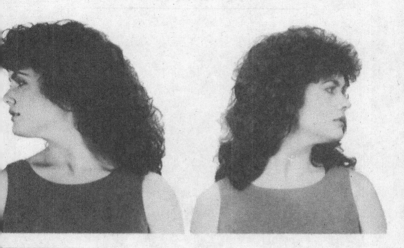

❏ Repeat as for Days 10-16.

NOTE: As your muscles relax even more, you will be able to curl up your pelvis more to stretch your spine and you won't have to bend your knees as much.

DON'TS

❏ **Do not turn your body or rotate your shoulders.**

❏ **Do not lock your knees.**

❏ **Do not tense your neck or shoulders.**

❏ **Do not stick out your buttocks or stomach.**

Repetitions TO EACH SIDE						
Day 17	Day 18	Day 19	Day 20	Day 21	Day 22	Days 23-30
4	4	4	4	4	4	4

BUILD YOUR STRENGTH

101

The Bent-Knee Reach

TECHNIQUE

❏ Repeat as for Days 10-16, but when you can't round any more, release your hands and extend your arms straight out alongside your legs, so that they are parallel to the floor. Try to keep your legs loose and relaxed.

NOTE: As you learn to round up even more, this will gently stretch your neck and the area between your shoulder blades, releasing tension in the back and letting you focus on working the stomach muscles only.

As you learn to relax, the rest of your body will feel like a rag doll. in addition, as your neck muscles stretch further, you may feel the muscles along the sides of your neck for a session or two. These are the muscles that make your neck look long and regal.

DON'TS

❏ **Do not rock your entire body back and forth.**

❏ **Do not tighten your buttocks.**

❏ **Do not bounce your head or aim it toward the ceiling.**

❏ **Do not hold in your stomach muscles.**

❏ **Do not hold your breath.**

❏ **Do not lift just your head first.**

❏ **Do not move just your arms.**

Repetitions						
Day 17	Day 18	Day 19	Day 20	Day 21	Day 22	Days 23-30
100	**100**	**100**	**100**	**100**	**100**	**100**

Single-Leg Raises

TECHNIQUE

DON'TS

❏ Do not tense your toes, knees, or legs.

❏ Do not bring the raised leg toward your head, but, rather, round your body toward your leg.

❏ Do not rock your body back and forth.

❏ Do not jerk up your head.

❏ Do not aim your torso towards the ceiling.

❏ Do not tense your stomach.

❏ Do not forcibly tighten your buttocks.

❏ Do not move only your hands and arms.

❏ Repeat as for Days 10-16, this time trying to round up even more and raising the extended leg several inches off the floor. Try to keep it perfectly straight and relaxed. Remember, move only ¼ to ½ inch.

❏ Work both sides.

NOTE: As you continue to get stronger, you will be able to round your nose even more into your rib cage, and this will work your stomach muscles even more.

Repetitions TO EACH SIDE						
Day 17	Day 18	Day 19	Day 20	Day 21	Day 22	Days 23-30
100	100	100	100	100	100	100

Double-Leg Raises

TECHNIQUE

❏ Repeat as for Days 10-16, very slowly lowering the legs toward the floor, no more than 4 inches.

NOTE: Now is when you will really start to see fast results, but be **sure** *not to lower your legs so much that your lower back comes into play.*

Start very slowly, lowering your legs ¼ inch at a time. Should you feel it in your lower back, come up ¼ inch at a time. Experiment carefully until you find the position that is comfortable—but challenging—for you.

DON'TS

❏ **Do not lift up your legs without bending your knees first.**

❏ **Do not tense your legs, knees, or toes.**

❏ **Do not jerk your neck.**

❏ **Do not tense your neck or shoulders.**

❏ **Do not move your body back and forth.**

Repetitions						
Day 17	Day 18	Day 19	Day 20	Day 21	Day 22	Days 23-30
100	100	100	100	100	100	100

105

Both Legs Over

TECHNIQUE

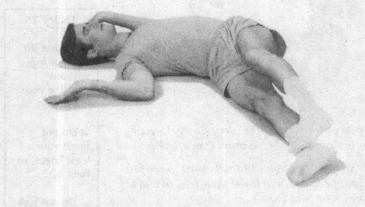

❑ Repeat as for Days 10-16.

NOTE: As you become more skilled, you will perform this stretch with greater ease. You will find that you will enter a more relaxed state even quicker. So, a word of warning: if you have somewhere to go or an appointment to keep, be very careful; you can relax so much that you fall asleep!

DON'TS

❑ Do not tense or jerk your body.

❑ Do not rush through this stretch.

Hold for a count of...						
TO EACH SIDE						
Day 17	Day 18	Day 19	Day 20	Day 21	Day 22	Days 23-30
60	60	60	60	60	60	60

Neck to the Side

TECHNIQUE

❑ Repeat as for Days 1-4.

NOTE: Now is when you will become fully aware of the tension in your neck and shoulders and will notice the discomfort it has been causing you. Just remember that you can undo years of tension in a few minutes each day.

Repetitions TO EACH SIDE						
Day 17	Day 18	Day 19	Day 20	Day 21	Day 22	Days 23-30
1	1	1	1	1	1	1

The Three-Quarter Neck Relaxer

TECHNIQUE

❏ Repeat as for Days 10-16. If your muscles are very tense, you will feel a stretch between your shoulder blades.

NOTE: Take advantage of this opportunity to be kind to your precious neck! You can perform neck relaxers in so many places: sitting at your desk, watching TV, showering, stuck in a traffic jam... do them and see. You'll feel more alive and so relaxed.

DON'TS

❏ **Do not force your head down.**

❏ **Do not tense your shoulders.**

Repetitions
TO EACH SIDE

Day 17	Day 18	Day 19	Day 20	Day 21	Day 22	Days 23-30
1	1	1	1	1	1	1

109